For the truly GREAT Phoebe Yeh!
—J.H.

To Nicole, the NICEST art director in this book!
—L.K.

Text copyright © 2021 by Joan Holub
Jacket art and interior illustrations copyright © 2021 by Laurie Keller

All rights reserved. Published in the United States by Crown Books for Young Readers,
an imprint of Random House Children's Books, a division of Penguin Random House LLC, New York.

Crown and the colophon are registered trademarks of Penguin Random House LLC.

Visit us on the Web! rhcbooks.com

Educators and librarians, for a variety of teaching tools, visit us at RHTeachersLibrarians.com

Library of Congress Cataloging-in-Publication Data is available upon request.
ISBN 978-0-525-64528-3 (hardcover)—ISBN 978-0-525-64529-0 (lib. bdg.)
ISBN 978-0-525-64530-6 (ebook)

The text of this book is set in Sugary Pancake.
The illustrations in this book were created using traditional and digital collage.
Book design by Nicole de las Heras

MANUFACTURED IN CHINA   10 9 8 7 6 5 4   First Edition

I AM THE SHARK

written by
Joan Holub

illustrated by
Laurie Keller

Crown Books for Young Readers ♕ New York

Hey there!

My name is Great White Shark.

I am the

GREATEST SHARK

IN THIS BOOK.

I am Whale Shark.
I am the greatest shark
in this book. Because I'm the
BIGGEST.
I'm as big as a school bus!
I'm the biggest fish on earth.
I'm so BIG, I don't even fit
on this page! Compared
to *me, you* are

small.

Interesting theory.
But being small is great
too. It means I can swim
through spaces where
you won't fit.
Plus, I don't
have to eat
as much as you.
Saves me time
on hunting.

Hooray!
I am the
SMALLEST shark
in this book.

No,
you're
not.

I'm the smallest. I'm only as big as a person's hand. Dwarf Lantern Shark is my name. Small and glowing, that's me. I can fit through even smaller spaces than **YOU.**

Hmm. I'm thinking that a tiny shark like you probably has a tiny brain. I'm smart and curious. Maybe I am the **SMARTEST** shark in this book!

Or maybe you're not.

I'm Hammerhead Shark. I've got a large brain between these eyes on both ends of my hammer-shaped head. And while I'm thinking smart thoughts, I can see up, down, and all around. I've got a better view of the ocean than any other shark!

Whoa!
How can I top that?

Top?
Hey, that's it!

I have a gray top (or back). Unsuspecting prey above me don't even notice me against the dark-colored water below me until . . . .

CHOMP!

Yet my tummy is white, so to prey
looking up from below me,
I blend in with the
lighter sky above.
This is called
countershading.

And it makes me the SNEAKIEST shark in this book!

No, you're not.

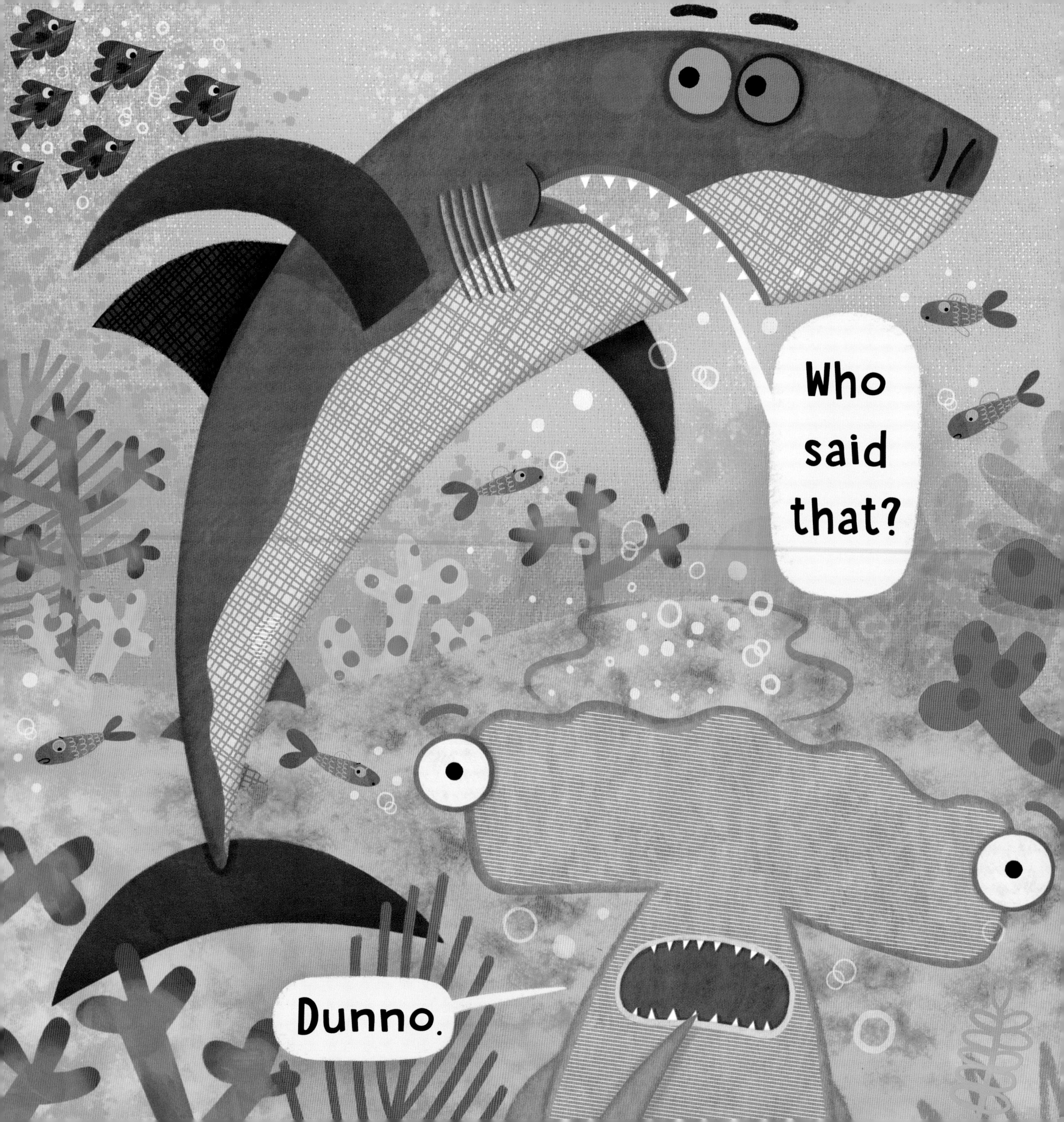
Who said that?
Dunno.

I am Angel Shark.
Camouflage makes *me* the
SNEAKIEST shark in this book.
My back is covered with spots,
so when I hid under the
sand just now, I looked like
part of the ocean floor.
Then woo-hoo . . .
AMBUSH!

Crumbs.

Guess I'm not the
sneakiest, after all.

Wait.
I know!
I'm great at finding
prey like seals,
sea lions, and
small whales.
I must be the best
HUNTER
in this book!

Nuh-uh.

I'm as good a hunter as you. Maybe better. I am Tiger Shark. I hunt animals like seals and squid, but there's a reason they call me the garbage can of the ocean. It's because I gobble other stuff too. One time I ate a clock and a car tire. True story.

It's better for the environment if garbage doesn't ever wind up in the oceans, though.

Sigh.
This being
one-upped is
getting old.

Old?
That reminds me . . .
I have been in this book
since the *very first page!*
So I must be the
OLDEST shark
in this book.

No, you're not.
I'm Greenland Shark.
And I am 400 years old.
No other animal with
vertebrae (a backbone or
a spine) can live longer than
that. So you are definitely
younger than me.

Okay, moving on.
Let's see—I've got
fins like a fish.

Maybe I am the
FISHIEST shark
in this book?

Let's review some shark facts.
Maybe it'll help me figure out the
greatest thing about me. Here goes. . . .

But first a little diagram of me, the
GREAT WHITE SHARK!
(Not all sharks have these same body parts.)

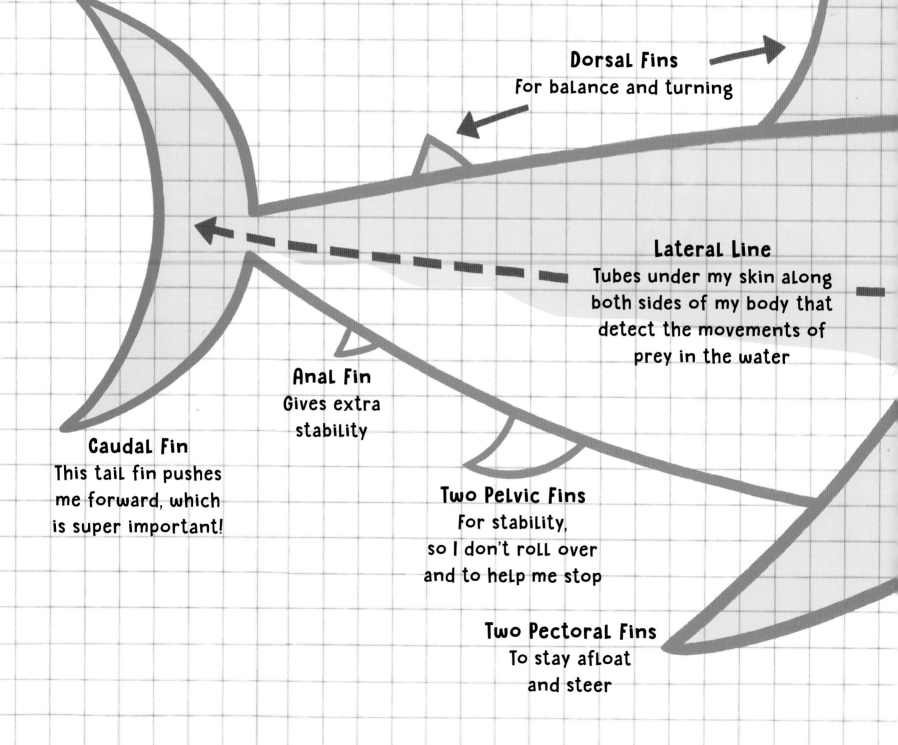

Dorsal Fins
For balance and turning

Lateral Line
Tubes under my skin along
both sides of my body that
detect the movements of
prey in the water

Anal Fin
Gives extra
stability

Caudal Fin
This tail fin pushes
me forward, which
is super important!

Two Pelvic Fins
For stability,
so I don't roll over
and to help me stop

Two Pectoral Fins
To stay afloat
and steer

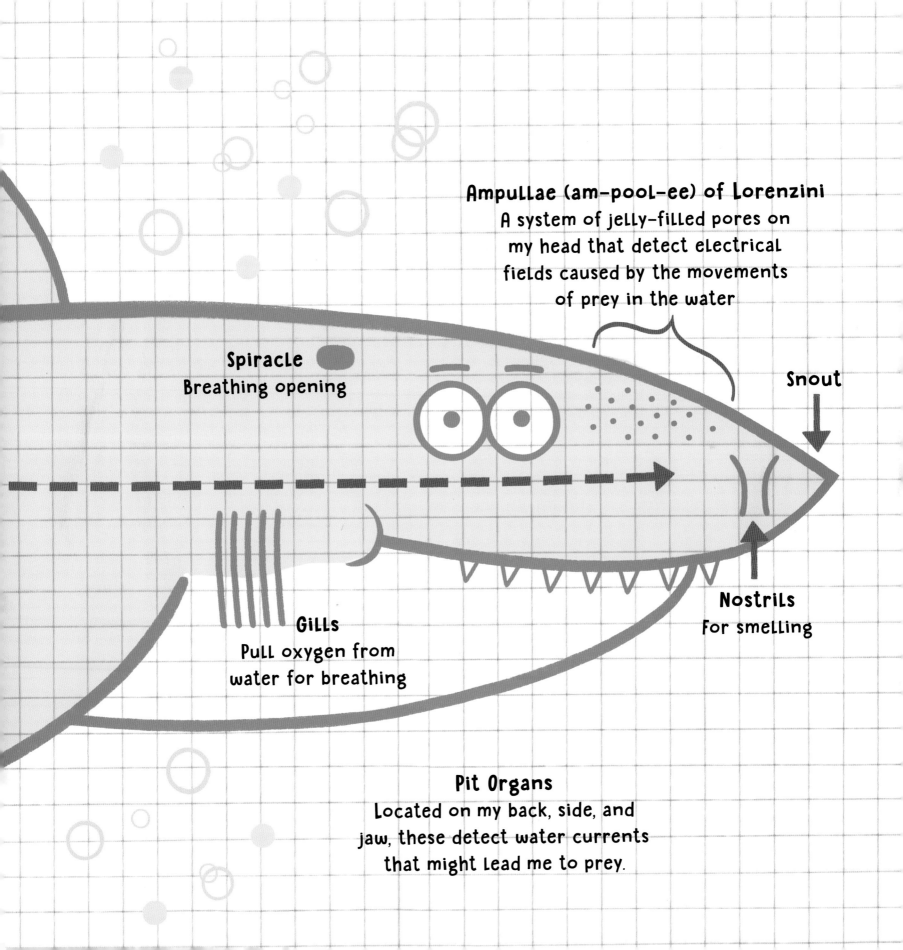

NOW FOR SOME *FIN*TASTIC SHARK FACTS:

Sharks are fish.
Most fish have bones,
but sharks don't.
Our skeletons are made of
cartilage (like people's ears).
It bends, so we can twist,
turn, and swim fast. It's
lightweight to help us float.

Sharks and people have
five senses: hearing, smell,
touch, sight, and taste.
Sharks also have these:
ampullae of Lorenzini,
lateral line, and pit organs,
which help detect electric
and magnetic fields,
temperature changes, or
even ocean currents.

Sharks have fins that act as
paddles. Tilting a fin helps
us to change direction,
move up, down, or forward,
or move slower or faster.

Some sharks, like the great
white, must keep swimming
to breathe underwater.
Water flows into our open
mouths as we swim.
Our bodies pull oxygen from
the water as it flows back
out of us through slits
in our sides called gills.

Female sharks are
usually bigger than
male sharks.

We have lots of teeth in rows. If a tooth falls out, no problem. Another one moves forward to take its place.

Some baby sharks hatch from eggs. But many shark moms give birth to live young sharks called pups. Newborn shark pups can swim right away.

Sharks are covered with tiny scales called denticles that protect us like a knight's armor. Our skin feels smooth if stroked from head to tail, but like sandpaper when stroked in the opposite direction.

Sharks have lived on Earth since before the dinosaurs!

Most sharks are meat-eaters called carnivores. We are amazing hunters. Predators—top of the food chain! We hunt and eat other animals called prey, such as fish or seals. Some sharks eat plants and tiny animals called plankton.

Speaking of food, I've got a feeling....

Woo-hoo!
I'm faster than those other sharks.
I am way ahead.
I'm going thirty-five miles per hour.
I am the FASTEST swimmer in this book!

SNACK ATTACK!
(30 to 50 feet away)
I SEE YOU!
Any minute now . . .
PREY AHEAD

I'm Mako,
the fastest
shark in this book!
I've been clocked
swimming forty-six
miles per hour.

**I WIN
THE PREY!**
Hooray!

ALL the other sharks in this book are better than me.

Could it be that I'm *not* the GREATEST?

Maybe I should change my name to Just-Okay White Shark or *Not-So-Great* White Shark.

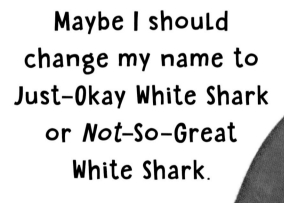

Dude . . . there's always going to be somebody that's bigger, smaller, glowier, smarter, sneakier, older, faster, or whatever. Just be happy being you.

HAPPY? That's it!

Everyone **LOVES** my big, bright smile.
They take my picture wherever I go.

I mean, who else do you know with 300 jagged,
triangle-shaped, two-inch-long pearly whites?

It's
awesome
to be
me.

I have the **GREATEST** smile in this book!

There are about 500 species (kinds) of sharks around the world. Most sharks live in saltwater oceans. But some of us like freshwater (non-salty) rivers. Our eating habits help keep oceans healthy by balancing how many and what kinds of creatures live there.

GREAT WHITE SHARK: Toothiest AKA Jaws

I'm named for my white tummy. I have the strongest bite of any shark. Unlike most sharks, I'm warm-blooded, so I can control my body temperature when I visit cool and warm waters. I'm fifteen to twenty feet long.

ANGEL SHARK: Sneakiest

I'm flat with winglike fins that make me look like a stingray. Unlike some sharks, I don't have to keep swimming to breathe. My cheek muscles and spiracles can pump in oxygen-rich water that exits through my gill slits. I'm about six feet long.

MAKO SHARK: Fastest

I'm shiny, like blue metal. I'm really good at leaping out of the water. That's called breaching. There are two kinds of makos, longfin and shortfin. I'm a shortfin. I'm about ten feet long.

HAMMERHEAD SHARK: Brainiest

I got my name because my head is shaped like a hammer. The location of my eyes lets me see in every direction, except right in front of my nose. I can measure up to twenty feet long.

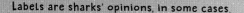
Labels are sharks' opinions, in some cases.

WHALE SHARK: Biggest

Most of the biggest sharks like me are filter feeders. My mouth is almost five feet wide. I swim with it open to let meals of small fish and tiny plants float inside. I'm about thirty to forty feet long.

DWARF LANTERN SHARK: Smallest

I'm bioluminescent. That means my body can change chemical energy into light energy that makes my fins and tummy glow. This helps me find food in the deep, dark ocean. I'm about seven inches long.

GREENLAND SHARK: Oldest

I swim very slowly, less than one mile per hour. I live in the cold Arctic near the top of the world and can dive deep, about 7,000 feet. I grow up to twenty-three feet long.

GREAT WHITE SHARK TOOTH, ACTUAL SIZE

TIGER SHARK: AKA Garbage Can

I have dark stripes like a tiger. I'm one of the most dangerous sharks, second to great whites. Shark attacks on people are very rare, though. I'm ten to fourteen feet long.

BEAR SHARK: Furriest

I'm a shark too!

No, you're not.

Wait, what?
Excuse me, but sharks do not
have fur. Or claws. So you are
not a shark. You seem cool and
all, but . . . you are a bear.
Obviously.
And a bear does not
belong in a shark book.

GRRREAT points.
I know!
I'll go find my own book to star in.
I will call it *I Am the Bear.*
I'll be the only bear inside it.
It'll be all about me, me, me, only me!
Awesome, pawsome.
Later, sharks!

MORE BOOKS TO SINK YOUR TEETH INTO!

Short ones:

Hark! A Shark! (The Cat in the Hat's Learning Library), by Bonnie Worth. New York: Random House, 2013.

Sharks (DK findout!). New York: DK Publishing, 2017.

Sharks (National Geographic Kids), by Anne Schreiber. Washington, D.C.: National Geographic Society, 2008.

Longer ones:

Shark Week: Everything You Need to Know, by Martha Brockenbrough. New York: Feiwel and Friends, 2016.

Sharks and Other Deadly Ocean Creatures Visual Encyclopedia. New York: DK Publishing, 2016.

Sharks: Facts at Your Fingertips (DK Pocket Genius). New York: DK Publishing, 2016.

Links:

kids.nationalgeographic.com/animals/fish/

ocean.si.edu/ocean-life/sharks-rays/sharks

Don't swim too close to sharks. We can be dangerous. But we're helpful too. Our hunting skills help keep the oceans healthy. Still, we face problems like water pollution and getting caught in fishing nets. You can help us by telling others how important we are to the earth's oceans. Thanks, you are GREAT!